Seeking Foundation Grants

by Barbara Stewart Gary

**National Catholic
Educational
Association
Office of Development**

Table of Contents

1   **Foundations as a Funding Source**
3   Types of Foundations
4   Grantsmanship as a Process
5   Researching Foundations
6   Foundation Research Sources
8   How to Approach Foundations
9   Requesting an Interview
10   The Meeting
13   Packaging the Proposal
17   The Proposal

   Appendices
21   A. Sample Proposal I
27   B. Sample Proposal II
38   C. The Foundation Center

About the Author

Barbara Stewart Gary is the Director of *Business Leadership Organized for Catholic Schools* (BLOCS). Initiated in 1980 by a non-sectarian group of Philadelphia business leaders, BLOCS serves as the development effort for the 282 schools of the Archdiocese of Philadelphia. To date, over $28 million has been raised by the BLOCS program.

From 1980-85, as part of her responsibilities as Director of the BLOCS program, Mrs. Gary researched and wrote capital and program-related proposals which generated more than $7.5 million in foundation grants. During this period she met with officers of many major foundations (independent and corporate; local and out-of-state), for the purpose of clarifying the scope and case for support of the Catholic Schools.

Mrs. Gary has contributed articles to *Proeducation Magazine* and *Momentum*. In addition, she has conducted development related workshops and seminars for schools, dioceses and religious communities throughout the country, and is a past and future participant at the NCEA development symposium.

Before assuming the Directorship of BLOCS, Mrs. Gary taught for nine years in the Philadelphia Archdiocesan Secondary School System, serving as Chairperson of the Social Studies Department at Archbishop Wood High School for Girls in Warminster, Pennsylvania from 1976-1980.

Mrs. Gary holds a Bachelor of Arts degree from St. Joseph College, Emmitsburg, Maryland and a Masters degree in Science from Temple University.

Mrs. Gary resides in North Wales, Pennsylvania with her husband, Stephen, who is the Vice Principal of Archbishop Wood High School for Boys. They have two sons.

Foreword

While foundations are one of the four major sources of giving available to Catholic institutions, they are the least understood. Many administrators and development directors shy away from developing relationships with potential foundations because of a feeling of uncertainty. This behavior has many times left worthwhile foundations out of the funding cycle of programs which would meet the foundations' goals.

Barbara Stewart Gary describes a very understandable and workable *process* which can be used to develop a relationship with a foundation. She shares a great deal of practical down-to-earth information about the life of foundations and the most practical methods available for relating to them. *Seeking Foundation Grants* contains practical step-by-step suggestions for identifying foundations, preparing a proposal and delivering the project to the foundation's consideration.

I am delighted to introduce this "how to" book to our development series and to publicly thank Mrs. Gary for her development work on behalf of Catholic institutions not only in Philadelphia but throughout the nation.

Reverend Robert J. Yeager
Vice President/Development
October 15, 1985

Seeking Foundation Grants

Barbara Stewart Gary

I n Carol Kurzig's book, *Foundation Fundamentals: A Guide for Grant Seekers,* she reports that a California foundation, while analyzing its previous year's grants, found that it funded only 1.9 percent of all the proposals it received. (A very discouraging statistic if you're attempting to apply for a foundation grant.) The same foundation, however, also found that over 90 percent of all the proposals it received were totally outside its stated and widely publicized scope of interest. This is not an unusual case. The majority of foundation proposals are rejected because the applicants simply do not understand how foundations make grants.

For a better understanding of the grantmaking procedure, we need to begin with a better understanding of foundations themselves.

Foundations as a Funding Source

Foundations are but one of four major sources of philanthropic giving available to your school, parish or diocese. They include:

- Individuals
- Foundations
- Corporations
- Bequests

In 1984, $66.44 billion or 89.5% of all charitable dollars in the United States came from individuals (including bequests). Foundations were responsible for 5.8% or $4.36 billion. Total contributions from corporations amounted to $3.45 billion or 4.7%. These percentages should remain relatively constant over the next few years.

Since 1981, the tax law governing foundation earnings has been changed. Foundations are not required to expend all the earnings on their assets, but may channel some of these earnings back into the capital assets which generate those earnings. Foundation officials promise that this will be more beneficial to grantseekers in the long run, enabling foundations to build up their size and grantmaking capabilities in the future.

While private foundations by-and-large are dependent on their assets to make grants, corporate giving is largely dependent on corporate profits. How much a company can give, and whether that giving will go up or down is very much dependent on how much the company makes. The more profitable a company, the greater its philanthropic potential.

This leaves individuals. Whereas corporations have to justify their giving to various constituencies, private individuals can freely dispose of their income. Individuals produce two, out-of-every three philanthropic dollars in America. They are historically responsive to well-educated appeals, and, at least those in the middle to upper income ranges, have generally had a more favorable immediate impact from current economic programs.

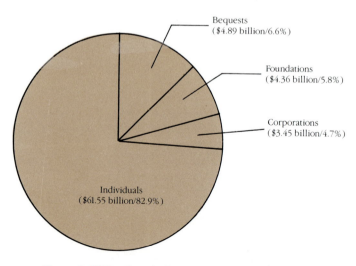

Bequests
($4.89 billion/6.6%)

Foundations
($4.36 billion/5.8%)

Corporations
($3.45 billion/4.7%)

Individuals
($61.55 billion/82.9%)

Figure 1 Philanthropic Giving in the United States

One additional note—individuals also run corporations and sit on foundation boards. A ripple effect, therefore, may be expected from their successful cultivation. Individuals are also more likely to give to religious education programs per se and to religious owned and operated schools.

With these figures in hand, you may question whether your institution should even bother applying for foundation grants. Keep in mind, however, that over 500,000 grants are made annually, and that 2,800 foundations make individual grants of $100,000 or more. Even more encouraging is the fact that increasingly more attention is being paid to elementary and secondary education (and private education) by the foundation world. My own belief is that foundations are worth the investment of time and energy and are a viable funding source for Catholic schools and dioceses.

Types of Foundations

The Foundation Center defines a foundation as "a non-governmental, non-profit organization with funds and programs managed by its own trustees or directors, and established to maintain or aid social, educational, charitable, religious or other activities serving the common welfare, primarily through the making of grants."

There are basically three types of private foundations and one type of public foundation which are of interest to grant-seekers. The three private foundation types include:

Independent—a foundation that receives its funds from a single person, a few individuals or a family. Depending on the subject range of their giving, independent foundations may also be classified as "general purpose" or "special purpose" foundations. Independent foundations can be either national or local in terms of the geographic area served.

Corporate—a foundation created by a profit-making business to support non-profit institutions. Topics of interest are often related to corporate interest.

Operating—a foundation that uses funds given to it by others to operate its own programs, rather than granting funds to help other agencies to do so.

The public foundation type include:

Community Foundations—a foundation whose endowment comes from bequests and gifts from many donors.

Community Foundations generally make grants only in their own metropolitan area and are usually classified by the IRS as public charities. They are not subject to the same regulatory provisions that apply to private foundations. Often these foundations carry the name of the community they represent, for example: The Philadelphia Foundation and the Hartford Public Welfare Fund.

Grants- manship as a Process

The potential for getting a foundation grant depends on how much staff time can be directed to the foundation research and application process. Grantsmanship is a *process*, not just an exercise in proposal writing.

Shotgunning proposals to various foundations is not the right approach. Far too often grantseekers look at a foundation's assets and think that there has to be money there for me. Roughly 80% of these proposals are denied funding. Time and effort are wasted by simply writing proposals and sending them through the mail.

Foundations are attracted to well-defined, interesting projects, as opposed to requests for unrestricted monies or general support grants. The individual diocese, school or parish must, however, maintain its integrity when approaching foundations.

Be sure your proposals honestly reflect school or parish needs. Be careful not to let a foundation dictate what you ask

The Edna McConnell Clark Foundation located in New York City awarded $15 million in grants last year. At a recent development symposium in Philadelphia, John R. Coleman, President of the foundation, offered this advice to grantseekers:

"I think too many of you could sell any program without feeling any commitment to it. It seems critical to me that what you're doing should be something you believe in."

Good foundation proposals, like good development offices, are the result of the untiring efforts of committed people, who dare to dream and then seek the necessary resources to make those dreams realities.

Foundations are looking for partners. It's our task to demonstrate that Catholic schools, parishes and dioceses can provide the "perfect match."

for or change the direction of your institution's philosophy or long-range plan.

Ideally, the development office should serve as the coordinator and clearinghouse for all contacts with foundations. Proposals and correspondence about foundation grants should flow through the Development Office. An uncoordinated foundation-solicitation effort could not only prove embarassing to your institution, but could also delay the achievement of projects that are most necessary to the success of your long-range plan. The Development Office has the responsibility of working with department heads and staff to formulate proposals which address school or parish needs. To find out which foundations will most likely fund these particular projects demands that adequate time be spent researching foundation prospects.

Researching Foundations

The Development Office should prepare a list of foundations to be researched and contacted in a given year. Yearly goals for foundation grants should be stated not only in terms of the number of foundations approached, but also in dollar amounts as well. For example, School X has program and capital needs totalling $25,000 for the current school year. The Development Office plans to approach six area foundations which make average grants of about $10,000. These figures will be adjusted according to the needs of the school and the grantmaking capabilities of the foundation. In this way a purposeful and effective approach to foundations can be initiated and followed.

A word of encouragement to those schools and parishes which do not have formal development offices. You will find that a faculty member, administrator or volunteer can successfully serve as a foundation researcher and liaison. In the case of a faculty member, a certain amount of scheduled "release time" during the day could be given to this designated grantseeker for the purpose of researching and developing foundation contacts. In the case of individual elementary schools and parishes, the best foundation prospects will be those located in your immediate area. The number of foundations which need to be researched for the most part, therefore, will be fewer than those available to a secondary school or diocese. Aside from this one restriction, however, all of the suggested procedures and guidelines for coordinating a foundation effort are applicable to the parish, diocese, elementary or secondary school. Begin your research by identifying:

- The largest foundations in the United States;
- The largest foundations in your state;
- The largest foundations in your state that demonstrate an interest in your area;
- The largest foundations outside your state that demonstrate an interest in your area;
- Smaller foundations in your community that have an interest in your area.

Thoroughly investigate each foundation in terms of:

- The size of grants made. (You will be given a range here—be careful to stay within it.)
- Geographic location
- Type of support given, (capital funds, endowment, scholarship assistance)
- Type of recipient, i.e., higher education, churches, seminaries, private schools or public schools.

Foundation Research Sources

Information about foundations can be found in a number of reference materials. The Foundation Center in New York is the most comprehensive source of information on foundations and has more than eighty regional locations in all fifty states, Mexico and Puerto Rico.* These regional centers are usually located in local library facilities. The address of the center nearest you can be obtained from The Foundation Center, 888 Seventh Avenue, New York, New York 10019 or by calling 800-424-9836.

The Foundation Center provides the following recommended research materials:

The Foundation Directory—A reference book published every two years by The Foundation Center. It lists, by state, approximately 3,000 foundations with assets of $1 million or more, and includes the name, address and telephone number of each foundation as well as the purpose, activities, trustees and contact person's name.

National Data Book—The only directory that includes all of the currently active grantmaking foundations in the United States. It lists over 22,000 foundations in one volume. Foun-

---

*See Appendix C.

dations are arranged by state in descending order of their annual giving totals, making it easy to gather information on foundations and their giving patterns by geographic area. City names are highlighted to help you identify the small foundations in any community.

Source Book Profiles —An annual subscription service offering in-depth profiles of the top 1,000 private and corporate foundations. It identifies a foundation's giving by type, amount, area and recipient. The service operates on a two-year publishing cycle, with each one-year series covering 500 foundations.

Foundation Grants Index Annual—A reference which identifies the kinds of organizations and programs the major foundations have been funding. The annual volume lists over 21,500 grants of $5,000 or more awarded by over 400 foundations. The volume is arranged alphabetically by state, then foundation name. Each entry includes the amount and date of the grant, name and location of the recipient, a description of the grant, and any known limitations in the foundation's giving pattern. It includes an index to grant recipients by name, an index to subject keywords and phrases, and a combined geographic and subject category index.

Comsearch Printouts—Computer produced guides to foundation grants of $5,000 or more, awarded by over 400 major foundations. Printouts list grants made in a particular subject area or geographic area.

Use the information provided on return that each foundation must file with the Internal Revenue Service; these include the 990 AR and the 990 PF. These files are available on all private foundations. Also check to see if the foundation publishes its own annual report. Many foundations do, and are willing to provide them along with any written guidelines they might have.

Having a good foundation reference library does not mean that an institution must purchase all of the recommended books, but as various sources are consulted and found useful, consideration should be given to permanently acquiring them.

Periodicals for your research activities may include a combination of the following:

- *Foundation News: The Journal of Philanthropy* published six times a year by the Council on Foundations, 1820 L Street, N.W., Washington, DC 20036.

- *The Grantsmanship Center News* published six times a year by the Grantsmanship Center, 1031 S. Grand Avenue, Los Angeles, California 90015.
- *The Philanthropic Digest* published sixteen times a year by Institutional Advancement Consultants, Inc. (1100 17th Street, N.W., Suite 912, Washington, DC 20036)

Learn to scan newspapers and local business periodicals for announcements of grants made by private and corporate foundations to various non-profit organizations. Keep a notebook of these press releases. This data will help you later in determining the size and type of grant a particular foundation is currently making.

After you have adequately researched the largest foundations available to you and your project, further refine the list by designating those that will receive primary attention in this calendar year and those which will receive secondary attention. Be sure you approach your local foundations first. Out-of-state foundations will expect you to have "home-town" support before you take your requests "on the road."

National foundations will more than likely ask you to substantiate local support for your institution's programs.

How to Approach Foundations

A good way to approach a foundation is from the perspective of someone who has something to offer them. Do not beg or plead; nor should you act as though you are entitled to the money simply because you have a worthy mission. Instead, you are approaching this funding source with an idea that you are convinced will serve the community and your constituency. Quite possibly your idea may address a regional or even national problem. Based on its previous/current interest in this area, you believe, the foundation may want to join your effort.

When you approach a foundation as a funding source much more depends on you. You must qualify your competency by means of letters, phone calls and interviews. Never submit a proposal until you have had an opportunity to meet face-to-face with a foundation official or, at the very least, have the chance to communicate with them over the telephone or by letter. Ideally, you should aim for a personal interview with the foundation official. If this is not possible, (and in many cases, foundations with small staffs will not grant initial interviews) carefully prepare your inquiry for delivery over the telephone or by letter.

Request- ing an Interview

By Telephone

When requesting an interview by telephone the following suggestions should prove helpful:

- Do your homework—Have the right name of the individual you wish to meet.
- Have pertinent information about your project at your fingertips.
- If possible, mention the name of a person known to the foundation, who may be connected with your institution or project.
- Be positive, convincing and enthusiastic, but not pushy.
- Keep it simple—no longer than two minutes. Answer questions, but suggest it would be easier to do so in person.
- Suggest a 15 minute meeting—"I will be in town in the near future. Can we set a date for an appointment?"
- In the event an interview is not possible, have questions ready. Give a distinct characteristic about your institution such as "The largest diocesan school system" or "The oldest parish in the city," then highlight the achievement or work of your school or parish and the one or two projects you envision for the foundation's support.
- Keep in mind that a tentative meeting is better than no meeting.
- If they say no money available now, don't sound down-hearted. Ask for their comments and reactions to your program. Seek some indication that the door would be open to a request at a future time.
- Write a memo for the record confirming the call and appointment (for internal use only).

By Letter

Beware of sending brochures or annual reports at this time. Instead submit the following:

- Write a short and simple one page letter. Indicate something which establishes your credibility. It may simply be your letterhead or a total budget figure for your parish or school system.

9

- Do not include a written proposal. Include information about your institution's work, scope and constituency and the project you envision for support.
- Include a list of gifts received to date or a list of other foundation grants received.
- List your board or key project people with title, if possible.
- Close with a restatement of your request for an interview.
- Indicate that *you* will call for an appointment.

The Meeting

Whom should you take with you? In part, it depends on the amount you're applying for—the larger it is, the more important should be the people who attend. You may wish to bring along an expert, if the project you intend to submit is very technical.

Be prepared for intense questioning. Hold dress rehearsals with your program people and staff beforehand. Answer all questions candidly. The grantsmanship process involves communication between the representatives of your school, parish or diocese and the foundation's staff. The dialogue that follows should be honest and open. For example, if your enrollment is dropping, say so. But counteract your figures by explaining the ways you're working to improve recruitment techniques and retention efforts.

Keep in mind that a foundation is people giving to people. Be down-to-earth with your request. Ask questions. Solicit advice. Be sensitive to the needs and concerns of the foundation—it, too, has a mission and a purpose.

During the meeting find out when the foundation board meets and what the deadlines for application are. Ask about format, length, and number of copies to be submitted.

Extend an invitation for an on-site visit by representatives of the foundation.

As a follow-up to your meeting, send a personal thank you letter, taking the opportunity to summarize the direction you were given during the visit.

In keeping with a development office's need to operate efficiently and effectively, it is advisable to file reports on all foundation contacts. Figure 2, which follows can be used internally and also shared with school board or parish council members when appropriate.

OFFICE OF DEVELOPMENT
FOUNDATION CONTACT REPORT
(Please type or print)

Name of Foundation _____

Address _____
         (street)

_____
     (city)   (state)   (zip)   (phone)

Executive contacted: (name and title) _____

_____

Date of contact: _____Method of contact: (visit, phone, other) _____

Purpose of contact: _____

_____

_____

Materials left with Foundation: _____

_____

_____

Additional materials to be submitted: _____

_____

_____

Is XYZ Institution on Foundation's mailing list? _____If not, was request made? _____

Development personnel who made this contact: (name and title) _____

_____

Name and title of person to whom grant requests should be directed: (Explain) _____

_____

Is there a specified method of making a grant application? _____

_____

Is there an optimum month or time of the year for submitting grant applications to ensure quick consideration? (If

yes, specify) _____

_____

Is there a deadline or closing date for acceptance of applications? _____

What is current thrust of Foundation interest? _____

Does it make grants towards operating budgets? _____

This report prepared by _____Date _____

(continued)

Figure 2 Foundation Contact Report

11

FOUNDATION RELATIONS OFFICE ACTION:

Follow-up action indicated _____

_____

Follow-up action taken: (what and when) _____

_____

_____

Do we have Foundation's latest annual report on file? _____

Is Foundation on our mailing list?_____If not, date added: _____

Foundation directory checked? _____Letter of appreciation to appropriate Foundation executive _____
                                                                                              (date)

★ ★

COMMENTS: (For use of development person who made contact with Foundation)

_____

_____

_____

_____

_____

_____

_____

_____

_____

_____

_____

_____

_____

_____

_____

_____

_____

Figure 2 Foundation Contact Report *(continued)*

Once your proposal is developed, begin circulating a copy of the request and the names of the foundation officers among your own board members or parish council members for possible contacts at the appropriate time. A word of caution, however: a contact with a board member of a foundation no longer guarantees a grant. A well-researched proposal, for a project which is within the foundation's interest, must be presented to the foundation staff first. Don't bring the "big guns" until you have completed your presentation to these staff members, and *never* use a contact to go around the foundation staff.

Packaging the Proposal

Your proposal should be accompanied by a one page cover letter (see Figures 3 & 4) that will indicate what your project is, who it will benefit and how it matches the foundation's interest. The cover letter should be written on the institution's letterhead and signed by the principal/pastor/chief administrator and/or development officer. The tone of the letter should be positive and professional.

You are attempting to convey your organization's credibility in a single page; avoid any reference to emergency conditions or dire need scenarios.

Unless otherwise directed, your proposal should be five to ten pages in length with supporting documentation and addendum attached.

All proposals should be accompanied by the following:

- Copy of the Internal Revenue Service Tax Exempt determination letter
- Names of Board Members, Development Committee or Officers
- List of any other pledges by source and amount
- Fact sheet.

Supporting documentation will vary from proposal to proposal. Some examples might be

- Drawings or diagrams
- Contractors' bids
- Enrollment projections
- Financial aid statistics
- Notices of awards or citations

August 21, 1985

Mr. John Jones
President
_____ Foundation
300 West West Street
Springhouse, California 10000

Dear Mr. Jones:

Based on the Foundation's interest in development related programs,
St. Joseph's High School seeks your support for a two year grant of
$63,200 to fund a Research Program for our Development Office. The
main purpose of the research program is to identify, research and
cultivate those select individuals (primarily alumni and parents) who
can provide the voluntary gift support essential for the survival of
a school like St. Joseph's.

Founded in 1894, St. Joseph's High School is a Catholic college-
preparatory school, serving 800 boys and girls in grades 9-12.
St. Joseph's School is owned and operated by the Sisters of St. Francis
and is financed solely by tuition and development-related programs.
In 1984, St. Joseph Academy surpassed its annual fund goal by
$40,000, raising $240,000 from its various constituencies.

As you probably know, development offices are new, in even
the best Catholic schools of the West. St. Joseph's High School
does not have a complete development program, but we are still
years ahead of most of our regional sister schools.

We are known for being helpful participants in the region.
Our recent workshop program on development for area high schools
bears this out; over 30 high schools participated in the two
day program.

Because we have been able to build a base of local support, we
are often visited by other Catholic school administrators beginning
their development work. As we seek to broaden our base of support,
we can continue to be a helpful resource for our colleagues in
other schools.

I hope that the _____ Foundation will support us, as we
attempt to take another important step in helping ourselves and
eventually helping many other schools in the region do the same.

Sincerely,

Sister Ann Margaret

Sister Ann Margaret
Principal

Barbara Gary

Barbara Gary
Director of Development

Figure 3 Sample Cover Letter

14

January 4, 1984

Mr. Charles Phillips
Senior Trust Officer
_____ Foundation

Dear Mr. Phillips:

Recognizing the contribution the _____ Fund has made to
civic and community life, and in particular, to Mercer County schools
and institutions, we are encouraged to seek its support for a capital
renovations project at Marian Catholic High School. The total cost
of the project is $100,000.

A brief look at this comprehensive, co-ed high school reveals
the following:

- A twenty-year old commitment to the educational and social
  climate of Mercer County;
- An enrollment of 2,501 students drawn from all income levels;
- A high academic, college and career-oriented curriculum with
  7 National Merit Finalists and 14 commendations in 1982;
- A dedicated staff which includes 178 Mercer County residents;
- A center for community activities and adult education;
- An estimated tax savings of $9,000,000 annually for Mercer
  County residents.

The major objective of this project will be to renovate and improve
existing facilities at far less than the cost of a new building.

Over the years, ever-mounting operational costs have not permitted
budget expansion in this area. Other projects involving scholarship
assistance and educational quality have taken precedence. An examination
of this building by outside experts, however, indicates that these
renovations are essential if Marian Catholic High School is to
continue to provide successful academic and recreational activities.

We would be pleased to conduct you on a tour of Marian Catholic
High School, and we welcome the opportunity to discuss our proposal
with you.

Sincerely yours,

Reverend Daniel Jones
Principal

Barbara Gary
Development Director

Figure 4 Sample Cover Letter

- Resumes of staff involved in the project
- Annual report (if available).

Submit the proposal well ahead of the given deadline for submission. In cases where the foundation is located in or around your city, it is wise to hand deliver it. This gives you and the foundation staff another opportunity for face-to-face contact and assures you that the foundation did indeed receive the proposal.

In cases where it is an out-of-state foundation, send the proposal certified mail. It's another minor detail, but one that could save you money in the end.

A Dozen Reasons Why Proposals Are Rejected

1. Problem has not been documented properly.
2. Problem does not strike reviewer as significant— failed to grab him or her.
3. Proposal is poorly written, hard to understand.
4. Proposal objectives do not match objectives of funding source.
5. Proposal budget is not within range of funding available through the funding agency.
6. Proposed program has not been coordinated with other individuals and organizations working in the same area.
7. Funding source does not know the capabilities of those submitting the proposal.
8. Project objectives too ambitious in scope.
9. Writer did not follow guidelines provided by funding agency.
10. Insufficient evidence that the project can sustain itself beyond the life of a grant.
11. Evaluation procedure is inadequate.
12. Methods unclear or inappropriate.

The Proposal

Begin your proposal by identifying the project for which you need funds and indicate the total cost of the project and the amount being requested from the foundation. Many grantseekers leave the requested amount for the budget page. By doing so, they commit a serious tactical error. The foundation knows you are coming to them for funds. The amount of funding, therefore, is the very first thing they will want to learn. Make sure it appears in the first paragraph of the first page.

In addition to conforming to the foundation's guidelines, interests and submission deadlines, the general quality of the proposal document is also a factor in the foundation's decision-making process.

Avoid the use of jargon or unidentified acronyms. Never include illegible photocopies or untitled graphs or charts.

Unsupported assumptions should be avoided. Thoroughly check for spelling errors or typos before submitting the finished copy. Care should also be taken to present the proposal in a clear, concise manner. For the most part, you should avoid using plastic covers and binders. Only include those attachments that significantly contribute to the clarity of the proposal.

The proposal should contain the following:

    I.   Introduction
    II.   Assessment of the Need
   III. Objectives of the Project
   IV. Method of Operation
    V. Evaluation
   VI. Budget
  VII. Plan for future funding of the project.

I. The Introduction

Use this paragraph to give a brief, comprehensive view of what is to be done by this project, whom it will benefit, and how it relates to the foundation's philosophy. Also indicate your institution's overall mission and goals in this introduction. This is also the place to state your institution's capability for implementing this project.

II. The Need

In this section of the proposal you should concentrate on identifying the specific problem or problems that will be addressed by the project. The definition of the needs should be narrowed down to the problem(s) you can hope to resolve within a reasonable period of time with the funds requested. Document the extent of the problems to be addressed by the project by including key statistical information. Charts, tables or graphs if essential to understanding of the problem, should be included in the addendum and simply referenced in this section. In summary, the problem or problems to be addressed by the proposed program should—

- Be stated clearly and concisely
- Be supported by appropriate documentation
- Have a reasonable expectation of being resolved by the proposed approach.

III. The Program Objectives

An objective is a specific, measurable outcome of the proposed project. Do not confuse objectives with methods of operation. Objectives are the *results* of the methods employed. The stated objectives of the program should clearly offer some relief for the problem or problems identified in the assessment of the need. Objectives should be stated in quantifiable terms. The proposal should indicate those quantifiable results expected for the entire program period and, if applicable, at periodic intervals throughout the proposed program period. Keep in mind that the foundation uses stated objectives as a key element in determining the basis for funding a proposed program.

IV. Method of Operation

This part of the proposal details how the proposed objectives will be achieved. This information should be presented in clear and concise terms. It must explain the operations of the program, identify, when possible, particular individuals who will perform certain functions and detail any other relevant data that will allow the foundation to evaluate the reasonableness of the proposed procedures and administrative controls.

As a minimum, this part of the proposal should include a statement on each of the following:

- *Area of coverage*—identify the specific geographic area served by the program.

- *Selection of participants*—describe the criteria for selecting those chosen for participation.
- *Administrative system and control*—define the lines of authority for the program. Attach job description if applicable.
- *Operational procedures*—describe the services to be provided.

In summary, this section should relate how the proposed operations will function to achieve the stated goals of the program.

V. Evaluation

This is a proposal element that many grantseekers overlook. A foundation will want to know that you have some kind of mechanism for checking the efficiency of your project. Both evaluation and the collection of basic data are extremely important if continued funding is to be sought from a foundation. It is advisable to develop a system whereby the results of the proposed program can be measured. This part of the proposal should include information on the following:

- *Impact of the program*—state what the expected impact of the program will be during the operation of the project as well as after the program is completed.
- *Data collection systems*—explain how information will be collected and used in the project's operation.
- *Evaluation and monitoring process*—explain how the program performance will be monitored, and by whom. Focus on the involvement of the administrative staff.

VI. Budget

A program budget is a coordinated plan of financial action to reach your stated objectives. The budget details how the funds you are requesting will be spent to achieve the goals and objectives of your proposal. Your projected figures, therefore, should be as specific and as accurate as possible. List the various expense categories to be charged against the program. Breakdown and itemize all projected expenses. Note any revenues/resources already allocated to the project from other sources.

Additional explanations about individual expense items can be attached on a budget justification sheet.

VII. Funding of the Program

Foundations usually want a beginning and an end to their involvement in a project. By the same token, they will also want to be assured that after their funds are expended the project will either be complete, (as in the case of capital renovations project) or aware of the plan that the institution has for raising the additional money to continue the project. You will find that many projects will become self-sufficient after a given period of time, as in the case of a development program project or teacher-training program.

If your proposal is to be brought to the foundation board, you may be asked to make various adjustments to the project or possibly to the budget. You may also be asked to respond to additional questions relating to your school or parish or to the project itself.

Appendices

A

Appendix

Sample Proposal I

PROPOSAL FOR THE EDUCATION/EMPLOYMENT PROGRAM
AT ST. FRANCIS ACADEMY

Submitted to:
XYZ Foundation
September 1, 1984

Submitted by:
St. Francis Academy
111 East River Avenue
New York, New York 10000

This is a request to the Officers of the XYZ Foundation for the funding of the Education/Employment Program at St. Francis Academy. The Education/Employment Program involves the updating and equipping of the clerical skills lab at St. Francis Academy at an estimated cost of $92,212, of which we are requesting $35,000 from the XYZ Foundation over a period of one year.

Founded in 1890, St. Francis Academy is owned and operated by the Sisters of St. Francis. The total enrollment of 552 girls makes St. Francis Academy the largest single-sex school in New York City. As an urban school, St. Francis Academy attempts to meet the needs of young women living in an urban environment. Of our students 60% are minorities; 38% are non-Catholic. At the present time 43% of the student body receive some type of tuition reduction. A student assistance profile of our student body is attached.

In response to the career needs of our students, St. Francis Academy adopted a long-range goal involving the development of advanced clerical and computer science programs. To achieve this goal, a substantial investment in automated office equipment and computers is needed.

More than 55% of the entire student body is enrolled in Business courses at St. Francis Academy.

The Education/Employment Program initiated in 1980 by Sister Clare Regan is cited as a model for urban schools.* The Education/Employment Program couples computer and clerical instruction with hands-on experience in local job settings.

New York Times, March 30, 1981.

The faculty and administration of St. Francis Academy are especially concerned for the future of our disadvantaged and minority students. Job-readiness today demands that our students be aware and comfortable with an automated office.

This is a major objective of The Education/Employment Program. Conversations with representatives of area corporations and industries indicate that exposure and mastery of advanced office machinery will give our disadvantaged students the competitive edge they need to succeed in the job market.

The Education/Employment Program at St. Francis Academy offers intense classroom training on advanced office machinery and basic business computers and word processors.

Approximately 70 to 80 students are placed in actual job settings. These students are selected and screened by the program administrators.

Students divide their day equally between school and job site. Employers work closely with the school personnel and the students. Job sites are secured by program administrators during the preceding school year. Evaluation of the program's objectives and of student performance is conducted by teachers, employers and students.

In order to accomplish the overall goal of the project—the improvement of the occupational competency of female, minority and disadvantaged students the following program objectives have been established:

- Instruct students in the skills necessary to operate computers and various business machines.
- Give students hands-on experience in working with computers and business machines.
- Familiarize students with office situations which occur on a daily basis and instruct them in the conduct appropriate to the situation.
- Build students' self-esteem and self-confidence which is so necessary in order to market themselves successfully in the competitive job world.
- Apprise students of the excellent career opportunities in the computer and related fields.
- Give selected students the opportunity to experience an actual work experience before graduation.

The timeframe for the project will cover the entire school year—September to June.

The method of operation for the project is as follows:

- Students will complete skill mastery tests after each unit of instruction indicating acquisition of that unit's skill.
- Students will perform the following functions on the computer and/or word processor:
  † calculate payroll
  † alphabetize a list of any category
  † plan/calculate inventory
  † create, revise and print documents
- Students will gain experience operating business machines by performing functions on the calculator, dictaphone, keypunch, and mag card and memory typewriters.
- Students will participate in role-playing designed to build self-confidence when encountering an actual work experience, e.g.
  † Students will complete various mock employment forms to gain familiarity with such forms
  † Students will take part in mock interview sessions. Role-playing of the employer and employee to gain confidence when placed in an actual interview session will be encouraged.
- Students will see themselves on videotape in order to correct any inappropriate speech or habits.
- Students will listen to presentations by representatives of computer companies and area businesses indicating range of computer employment.
- Students will participate in an actual job experience in the afternoon after intensive job related training in the morning. Participating employers have agreed to provide afternoon jobs for students to gain "on the job" experience.

As stated previously, students, teachers and employers will be involved in the program evaluation. The following instruments/materials will be used in the evaluation process:

- Reports by the two instructors noting the strengths and deficiencies of the program and recommendations for future implementation.
- Evaluations by participating employers in the work experience part of the program noting the strengths and

23

deficiencies of the program and recommendations for future implementation.

- Student questionnaires indicating how self-confidence and self-esteem increased as students progressed through the program.

According to the Department of Commerce surveys, those whose jobs involve the processing and communication of information now account for more than 50 percent of the work force. That number is expected to reach 65 percent by the year 2000. The already evident truth becomes obvious: the average person will find there are fewer jobs for unskilled workers. Without specific skills, our disadvantaged urban students who just get by in our present culture, will not survive in subsequent cultures. Intense, pre-employment training as offered in the Education/Employment Program encourages the disadvantaged child, who is often the below-average student, to pursue a practical and interesting career. The program offers incentive for the below-average student to remain in school, and provides the discipline and attitudinal training necessary for future job-related responsibilities.

In struggling to keep tuition costs down, budgetary restraint has been exercised in the purchasing of business machines and computers. At the present time 2 percent of the high school's $1.5 million operating budget is allocated to curriculum equipment.

The importance and timeliness of this project has made it a major objective of the development program for St. Francis Academy. Other contributions to this program as it exists at St. Francis Academy are listed on the attached sheet.

The equipment and updating of these labs will be interpreted as a tangible investment in the life and lives of the community St. Francis serves.

We welcome the opportunity to discuss our proposal with you.

Respectfully,

Sr. Elizabeth Marie
Principal

Barabara Gary
Director of Development

PROPOSAL I
EXHIBIT A—Detailed Budget

Quantity	Equipment	Cost per Item	Total Cost
2	TRS-80 Model III 48K	2,495.00	4,990.00
8	TRS-80 Model III 16K	1,000.00	8,000.00
5	Line Printers LP VIII	800.00	4,000.00
5	LP VIII Covers	5.00	25.00
10	Model III Covers	8.00	80.00
5	Line Printer Cables	40.00	200.00
5	Ribbon & Paper for Printers (each center)	200.00	1,000.00
20	Blank 5¼" Disks	4.00	80.00
5	Microcomputer Software Packages (Each containing the following:	980.00	4,900.00
	1 general ledger $100.00		
	1 inventory control 100.00		
	1 accounts payable 150.00		
	1 accounts receivable 150.00		
	1 disk payroll 200.00		
	1 manufacuring inventory control 200.00		
	1 fixed asset accounting 80.00)		
4	Manual — Introduction to BASIC	160.000	640.00
4	Workbooks	65.00	260.00
4	BASIC Programming Texts	200.00	800.00
4	Workbooks	99.00	396.00
10	TRS-80 System Desk	179.00	1,790.00
5	Universal Printer Stand	99.00	495.00
2	IBM Display Writer System, Single Station, 15 CPS Printer, double diskette 6580/A03, 224K	9,795.00	19,590.00
2	5608/TR3 Textpack III	725.00	1,450.00
4	Electric IBM Selectric III #6705	879.00	3,516.00
	TOTAL EQUIPMENT COST		$52,212.00
	Salaries and Benefits—2 Teaching Personnel		40,000.00
	TOTAL COST		$92,212.00

PROPOSAL I
Exhibit B—Scholarship Assistance Profile 1985-86 Results

#Applicants	Equipment Status	Requests
17	Truly Poor—less than $3,000 per person total family income*	$33,955
40	$3,000-$5,000 per person income	$47,240
14	$5,001-$6,000 per person income	$16,765
17	$6,001-$7,000 per person income	$18,230
6	$7,001-$8,000 per person income	$ 5,950
9	$8,001-$9,000 per person income	$ 9,620
3	$9,001-$10,000 per person income	$ 2,875
6	$10,000+ per person income	$ 4,525
		$139,160

*$10,000 total income/2 person family = $5,000 per person

B

Appendix

Sample Proposal II

RENOVATION OF SCIENCE LABORATORIES
AT HOLY CROSS SCHOOL*

Submitted to:
ABC Foundation
August 1, 1983

Submitted by:
Holy Cross School
4950 Dauphine Street
New Orleans, Louisiana 70117

This is a request for a gift of $50,000 to be spread over a period of three years, if you desire, for the renovation of Holy Cross' Chemistry, Physics, and Biology laboratories.

The total cost of the renovations estimated by Blitch Architects would be $250,000.00. (Please refer to the attached cost breakdown for details.) We feel this gift would greatly aid in stimulating the other members of the Holy Cross Family (alumni, parents, and friends) to contribute.

In reviewing this proposal, you may wish to consider the following points:

1. The renovations would begin as soon as possible and would have a completion date of August 30, 1983. This would enable the work to be accomplished during the summer months when the labs are not in use.

2. The money would be borrowed from a lending institution using the pledges as collateral with a pay-back period of three years. In this way the renovations will be completed as soon as possible.

3. The Holy Cross Science Department offers an impressive selection of elective classes in addition to required courses.

4. No science education program can achieve its full potential without adequate lab facilities. Presently, the science labs at Holy Cross are inadequate and outdated. They were constructed over 30 years ago. The plumbing system is now in such a condition which makes repairs impossible, and the electrical system is not sufficient for the types of experiments being performed in today's science class. Equipment and supplies must be upgraded as befits a properly outfitted laboratory for the 1980's.

5. Spacious, attractive, functional multi-purpose learning centers will enable us to provide courses receiving

---

*Reprinted with permission by Charles Biange, Assistant Headmaster, Holy Cross School, 4950 Dauphine Street, New Orleans, Louisiana 70117

27

more laboaratory experience with no wasted classroom space.

6. We will be better equipped to handle planned increases in student enrollment as well as additional sections of popular science electives.

The role that science plays in education at the secondary school level has changed greatly in the last ten years. Advances in science and technology have placed pressure on science educators to keep pace with changing conditions.

Holy Cross has a fine program of science education. Renovated laboratory facilities will greatly increase our effectiveness. Many of our graduates attending college enroll in curriculums in the fields of science, engineering, or pre-med, where first class experience is a necessity. These new facilities will improve their background experience. Our goal is not only to provide and extensive science background for those students, but also those who do not major in science on the college level.

At Holy Cross the task of preparing students to better face the challenges of modern society has done well in spite of our antiquated facilities. The 1982-83 Senior Class has seven National Merit Semi-Finalists, with two others narrowly missing that distinction, and the Scholastic Aptitude Test composite score for all 245 juniors was four points above the Louisiana average and two points above the national average. Improved facilities will improve our student's scientific background.

The enclosed suggested lab renovations and equipment lists were designed entirely by our science faculty. They conducted many studies and then agreed on the designs which they feel would best enable them to be most effective in their teaching.

We have enclosed for your information a copy of the science curriculum as well as a brief history of Holy Cross School.

The entire faculty is very excited about this project. We know you will give it careful consideration. We are hopeful that after reviewing the proposal, you will act favorably on it.

Sincerely in Holy Cross,

Br. John T. McLaughlin, C.S.C

Brother John T. McLaughlin, C.S.C.
Headmaster

BJTM:jg
Enclosures

PROPOSAL II

Exhibit A—History

The Brothers of Holy Cross are the oldest religious order of teaching Brothers in the United States. In 1842, the first of the religious came to America from France. They settled in Indiana, and with the priests of Holy Cross founded the University of Notre Dame.

In 1849, at the invitation of the Most Reverend Anthony Blanc, Archbishop of New Orleans, five Brothers arrived in New Orleans to assume the direction of St. Mary's Orphanage for Boys. One of this group was Brother Vincent, C.S.C., a founder of Notre Dame. In 1859, the Congregation purchased the site on which Holy Cross now stands; and in 1879, a boarding and day school was opened called St. Isidore's College. The foundation was a modest beginning, sprung from hard labor, suffering, and love of God. But its establishment was secure and firm, fashioned from the wills of men dedicated to the desire of bringing the teaching of God and men to the youth of the South.

The school grew quickly. On June 20, 1890, the General Assembly of the State of Louisiana chartered the institution, empowering it to confer degrees.

Five years later, when the present administration building was erected and solemnly dedicated, the name was changed to Holy Cross at the suggestion of the Most Reverend Francis Janssens, Archbishop of New Orleans. Soon, expansion of facilities became imperative; and in 1912, two wings were added to the main building to accommodate the steady increase of students, and a gymnasium was built. About the same time, the school, though chartered as a college, became a secondary institution, confining itself entirely to activities on that level. Since 1955, six modern facilities have been added to the campus at a cost of $2.6 million: the Upper School classroom building, the Student Center, the Brothers' Residence, a junior Olympic swimming pool, a new Student Residence, and a new Central Services Building. In addition, the Administration Building has recently undergone extensive restoration and renovation to make the facility more functional for modern educational methods.

PROPOSAL II

Exhibit B—Description of Project

The renovations will involve three classrooms (rooms 204, 208, and 209) presently used for laboratory experiments. We will begin with Room 204 for the following reasons: In this room there are tables which do not have running water and electricity, and they are in such configuration that the room cannot be used as a lecture room. The recommendation by the science faculty is to replace the tables with new ones which would have water, gas, and electricity and place them in a new configuration which would allow the room to be used *both as a laboratory and as a lecture classroom.* This would free seven additional sections of classroom space, which will relieve overcrowding in other parts of the school. In essence, it would be similar to building a new classroom without constructing a new building.

The lab situation in Rooms 208 and 209 present a different problem than the one in Room 204. They are crowded and lack proper storage space. Lectures are most difficult to present. For these reasons, the science faculty has recommended the configuration drawn by Blitch Architects, Inc. This configuration will allow teachers to conduct labs in the areas of Biology, Chemistry, or Physics. It will reduce crowding by dispersing students using the new stations along the walls. Storage space will be greatly increased with the additional storage below the student stations. The addition of a desk area in Room 209 for lecture *or* lab, thus freeing other classrooms for four periods a day. Adding these four sections to the seven sections obtained by the renovations to Room 204, will provide an additional eleven sections of classroom space.

The renovations not only will help upgrade our laboratory capabilities, but will add much needed space because of our increasing enrollment.

PROPOSAL II

Exhibit C—Cost Estimate

HOLY CROSS SCIENCE DEPARTMENT RENOVATIONS

CN-7910 COST ESTIMATE

A. Renovation Cost (includes Demolition)

    3,195 S.F. @ 56/S.F. $179,000.00

B. Fixed Equipment (Student Lab Tables, etc.)   47,000.00

C. Professional Fees

    (7% of A + B)   15,800.00

D. Contingency   8,200.00

           TOTAL $250,000.00

Equipment List—Physics

Quantity	Items	Per Item	Total
1	Vacuum Pump	$656.00	$656.00
2	Air Track	228.00	456.00
2	Air Table	253.00	506.00
6	Trajectory Apparatus	43.00	258.00
4	Air Supply	103.00	412.00
1	Vacuum Chamber	84.00	84.00
6	Ripple Tank	110.00	660.00
6	Wave Generator	13.00	78.00
6	Light Source (SK66457)	20.00	120.00
6	Optical Bench Kit	170.00	1,020.00
6	Light Source (SK69876)	25.00	150.00
3	Holography Kit	146.00	438.00
6	Resistance Unit	87.00	522.00
1	Oscilloscope	923.00	923.00
3	Power Supply	280.00	840.00
6	Voltmeter	75.00	450.00
6	Ammeter	75.00	450.00
6	Milliammeter	74.00	444.00
2	Electron Timer	255.00	510.00
2	Amplifier Power Supply	180.00	360.00
2	Oscillator Frey	126.00	252.00
2	Modulated Laser Frey	384.00	768.00
1	Stroboscope Frey	275.00	275.00
3	Polaroid Camera Frey	98.00	294.00
2	Wave Generator Frey	173.00	346.00
6	Resonance Apparatus Frey	60.00	360.00
1	Van de Graff	250.00	250.00
1	Discharge Electrode	40.00	40.00
5	Spectrum Tubes	15.00	75.00
	TOTAL (Physics)		$11,997.00

Equipment List—Chemistry

Quantity	Items	Per Item	Total
10	Electronic Blance	$1,795.00	$17,950.00
10	Triple Beam Balance	87.00	870.00
1	Electrolysis Apparatus	117.00	117.00
20	Burets 50ml	36.00	720.00
2	Centrifuge	180.00	360.00
1	Cork Boring Machine	145.00	145.00
2	pH Meter	440.00	880.00
1	Corning Mega Pure 1.4L Still	695.00	695.00
3	Hot Plates Magnetic Stirrer	253.00	759.00
3	Organic Chem. Glass Kit	225.00	675.00
1	Analytical Oven	875.00	875.00
1	Radioactivity Demonstrator and Experiment System	692.00	692.00
2	Spectrophotometer	875.00	1,750.00
1	Frost Free Refrigerator	750.00	750.00
	TOTAL (Chemistry)		$27,238.00

Equipment List—Biology

Quantity	Items	Per Item	Total
5	Wolfe IW3L Microscopes	$374.00	$1,870.00
2	Klima Gro 5000 Plant Ecosystem	564.00	1,028.00
1	IWK Inclined Microscope	596.00	596.00
2	20X Stereo Microscopes	498.00	996.00
1	Photomicrographic Camera & Adapter	323.00	323.00
1	Egg Incubator	146.00	146.00
1	Root View Growth Chamber	92.00	92.00
1	Resusci-Jane CPR Torso	546.00	546.00
1	70-5800 Ultrasonic Cleaner	320.00	320.00
2	Comprehensive Zoology Survey Lucite Cast	247.00	494.00
1	Articulated Human Skeleton (plastic) in Cabinet	496.00	496.00
10	Bane's Bacteria, Fungi and Plant Sets	30.00	300.00
10	Zoology Slide Sets	47.00	470.00
1	UV Insect Trap	95.00	95.00
1	Animal Cell Model	336.00	336.00
1	Ichikawa Color Blindness Test Booklet	54.00	54.00
1	Set Biology Specimens (plant & animal) embedded in Lucite	400.00	400.00
	TOTAL (Biology)		$8,562.00
	GRAND TOTAL (Equipment)		$47,797.00

PROPOSAL II

Exhibit D—Science Curriculum

General Science—Fifth and Sixth Grades

Modern science program entitled "Science: Understanding Your Environment" relates the study of environment to the everyday lives of children. Students are made aware that they are part of the environment and can act to preserve and improve it. Included in it is a balanced presentation of the biological, physical, and earth sciences. Students perform an abundance of activities and investigations in each of these three sciences. This program allows students to discover concepts through active inquiry.

General Science—Seventh and Eighth Grades

New system of science education developed by the Intermediate Science Curriculum Study. The program enables each student to work at his own pace in problems that grip his attention. A new integrated text-laboratory approach is used to involve students actively in science. Through this system students are provided with a generally useful foundation of powerful ideas and versatile skills needed for continued progress in science and for intelligent living in today's world.

Earth Science—Ninth Grade (elective)

Offered as a general survey course covering the most modern principles and concepts in earth science: rocks and minerals, erosion, earth history, earth structure, vulcanism and diatrophism.

Biology—Tenth Grade

Offered as a general survey course covering fundamental concepts in molecular and cellular biology: reproduction, genetics, and evolution; the protist, plant and animal kingdoms; the systems of man; and an introduction of ecology. Frequent lab sessions cover microbiology, taxonomic classification and dissection of representative specimens of the plant and animal kingdom.

Chemistry—Eleventh Grade

A survey course with five six-week periods of emphasis on basic inorganic chemistry and one six-week period of introductory organic chemistry. Text, films, and labs are combined to present the course.

33

Biology II—Eleventh and Twelth Grades (elective)

A second year biology course which deals specifically with the fields of oceanography, marine biology, and environmental science. Lab and field exercises that give the student an opportunity to experience what he learns in class are an integral part of the course.

Advanced Biology—Eleventh and Twelfth Grades (elective)

A lecture and laboratory study presented as a basis for the understanding of human anatomy and physiology. The anatomy section of the course will include detailed dissection of the cat and anatomical studies of other representative vertebrates. The physiology section will include the study of the physico-chemical processes in cells, tissues and organs of the human body. Prerequisites: The course is open to students on the junior and senior levels who maintained at least a "B" average in Biology I and/or approval of the instructor.

Advanced Chemistry—Twelfth Grade (elective)

This second year course is designed to emphasize college freshman sections of chemistry for the better science student. The five areas covered include: thermodynamics, chemical bonding, reactions, qualitative analysis and quantitative analysis. This elective course requires a "C" average in both math and science.

Physics—Twelfth Grade (elective)

A math-oriented study of the physical concepts of the world about us. The contents of the course are divided into six categories: 1) concepts of motion, 2) motion in the heavens, 3) mechanics, 4) light and electromagnetism, 5) the atom, 6) the nucleus.

Geology—Twelfth Grade (elective)

This course is designed to give the students an understanding of the methods of interpreting earth history as well as knowledge of the physical and biological history of the earth. Topics included are fossils and fossil preservation, evolution, uniformitarianism, plate tectonics, continental drift, and economic minerals and rocks.

Exhibit E—Science Department Personnel

Mrs. Sue Ellen Lyons, Science Department Chairman
Years Experience: 17
Subject Areas: General Science, Geology I (Physical), Geology II (Historical)
Degree: B.S. (Our Lady of Holy Cross College)
Science Credits: 47 hours
  Mrs. Lyons is currently a candidate for a M.A.S.T. degree (Master of Arts in Science Teaching), at the University of New Orleans.

Mr. Carl LaForge
Years Experience: 20
Subject Areas: Physics, Engineering Concepts, Algebra II
Degree: B.A. (Wichita State); M.S. (St. Louis University)
Science Credits: 24 hours

Mr. Chris Caboni
Years Experience: 17
Subject Areas: General Science, Biology II
Degree: B.S. (St. Edward's University); M.Ed. (Loyola University); +30 counseling (University of New Orleans)

Mr. Harold Reese
Years Experience: 17
Subject Areas: Biology, Anatomy and Physiology
Degree: B.S. (Southeastern Louisiana University)
Science Credits: 60+ hours

Mr. Al Wilhelm
Years Experience: 15
Subject Areas: Chemistry, Chemistry II
Degree: B.S. (Loyola University); M.Ed. Counseling (Tulane University)
Science Credits: 52 hours

Mr. John Sacco
Years Experience: 6
Subject Areas: Biology, Chemistry, Computer Science I and II
Degree: B.S. (University of New Orleans); M.Ed. (University of New Orleans)
Science Credits: 45 hours

Mr. Sacco has done original research for classroom purposes. The results of his study have been published in the December 1982 issue of *American Biology Teacher*. ("How Good Are Instant Bacteriological Media.")

Ms. Catherine Guidroz
Years Experience: 5
Subject Areas: General Science
Degree: B.S. (University of New Orleans)
Science Credits: 19
Mrs. Guidroz is currently working on a M.A.S.T. (Master of Arts in Science Teaching) degree at the University of New Orleans.

Mr. Paul Fradella
Years Experience: 5
Subject Areas: General Science
Degree: B.A. (University of New Orleans)
Science Credits: 18

Ms. Jill Burlingame
Years Experience: 3
Subject Areas: General Science, Biology, Chemistry
Degree: B.A. (Hartwick College)
Science Credits: 78

PROPOSAL II

Exibit F—Board of Directors

In 1980 the Holy Cross School, for the first time in its 102-year history, was governed by a board of directors comprised of Holy Cross Brothers and Christian laymen. The members of the board for the school year 1982-83 are as follows:

Chairman of the Board

Mr. Warren Deckert
Financial Consultant

Mr. Salvatore DiGrado
Dentist

Mr. A.J. Duplantier, C.P.A.
President
Duplantier, Hrapmann,
Hogan & Maher

Brother Fisher Iwasko, C.S.C
Local Religious Community
Representative

Mr. Malcolm Hurstell
Vice-President
New Orleans Public Service, Inc.

Mr. Ed Lee, Jr.
President
The Woodlands Development Corp.

Brother John McLaughlin, C.S.C.
Headmaster
Holy Cross School

Mr. Richard Crosby
Faculty Representative
Holy Cross School

Mr. John Sciambra
Attorney

Dr. Dan W. McCarthy
Associate Professor of
Chemical Engineering
Tulane University

Mr. Terry McCarthy
Sales Representative
Eli Lilly and Company

Dr. Tom Crais
Surgeon

Mr. Joseph C. Canizaro
Chief Executive Officer
Joseph C. Canizaro Interests

C
Appendix

The Foundation Center

The Foundation Center[1] has a nationwide network of reference collections for free public use which fall within four categories. The reference libraries operated by the Center offer the widest variety of user services and the most comprehensive collections of foundation materials, including all Center publications; books, services and periodicals on philanthropy; and foundation annual reports, newsletters and press clippings. The New York and Washington, D.C. libraries contain the IRS returns for all currently active private foundations in the U.S. The Cleveland and San Francisco field offices contain IRS records for those foundations in the midwestern and western states, respectively.

Cooperating collections contain IRS records for those foundations within their own state, and a complete collection of Foundation publications. Local affiliate collections provide a core collection of Center publications for free public use.

Some reference collections are operated by foundations or area associations of foundations. They are often able to offer special materials or provide extra services, such as seminars or orientations for users, because of their close relationship to the local philanthropic community. All other collections are operated by cooperating libraries or other nonprofit agencies. Many are located within public institutions and all are open to the public during a regular schedule of hours.

Please telephone individual libraries for more information about their holdings or hours. To check on the location of cooperating collections call toll-free 800-424-9836 for current information.

Where to Go for Information on Foundation Funding

Reference Collections Operated by The Foundation Center

The Foundation Center
Kent H. Smith Library
739 National City Bank Bldg.
629 Euclid
Cleveland, Ohio 44114
216-861-1933

The Foundation Center
312 Sutter Street
San Francisco, Calif. 94108
415-397-0902

The Foundation Center
888 Seventh Avenue
New York, New York 10106
212-975-1120

The Foundation Center
1001 Connecticut Avenue, NW
Washington, D.C. 20036
202-331-1400

---

[1]The Foundation Directory, 9th Edition. The Foundation Center, New York 1983, p. xxxiii.